D1538224

L. E. SMOOT MEMORIAL LIBRARY
9533 KINGS HIGHWAY
KING GEORGE, VA 22485

America's Game
Philadelphia Phillies

CHRIS W. SEHNERT

ABDO & Daughters
PUBLISHING

L. E. SMOOT MEMORIAL LIBRARY
9533 KINGS HIGHWAY
KING GEORGE, VA 22485

Published by Abdo & Daughters, 4940 Viking Dr., Suite 622, Edina, MN 55435.

Copyright ©1997 by Abdo Consulting Group, Inc., Pentagon Tower, P.O. Box 36036, Minneapolis, Minnesota 55435. International copyrights reserved in all countries. No part of this book may be reproduced in any form without written permission from the publisher. Printed in the United States.

Cover photo: Allsport
Interior photos: Wide World Photo: pages 1, 5, 8, 10, 13, 15-17, 20-23, 25-28.

Edited by Paul Joseph

Library of Congress Cataloging–in–Publication Data

Sehnert, Chris W.
  Philadelphia Phillies / Chris W. Sehnert
     p. cm. — (America's game)
  Includes index.
  ISBN 1-56239-664-1
  1. Philadelphia Phillies (Baseball team)—History—Juvenile
literature. I. Title. II. Series.
GV875.P45S45 1996
796.357'64'0974811—dc20   96-7598
                                     CIP
                                     AC

Contents

Philadelphia Phillies

In 1883, the Philadelphia Phillies baseball team joined the National League (NL). Ninety-seven years later, in 1980, the Phillies won their first World Championship.

The Phillies' history combines tales of misfortune with some of the greatest baseball players of all time. The Triple Crown pitching of Grover Alexander was later matched by that of Steve Carlton. From the hitting prowess of Ed Delahanty, to the hard-nosed style of Lenny Dykstra, Philadelphia fans have enjoyed some of baseball's most memorable moments, while suffering through more than their share of defeats.

The Phillies have had many great teams in their long history. All but one have fallen short of baseball's top honor. Today, the hard-luck Phillies continue their pennant pursuit.

Facing page: Philadelphia Phillies' Lenny "Nails" Dykstra bats in the 66th All–Star Game in Arlington, TX, July 11, 1995.

Wright Way

The Phillies finished last in their first season. They won only 17 of their 99 games, the lowest in club history. The following season, the Phillies hired Harry Wright to manage the team.

Wright is known as the "Father of Professional Baseball." His Cincinnati Red Stockings were the first openly professional baseball team, and he led the Boston Red Stockings to four NA Pennants in a row (1872-1875). In his 10 years as Phillies' manager, he brought the team to respectability.

The Phillies rose all the way to second place in 1887. They finished 3.5 games behind the Detroit Wolverines in the NL pennant race. Detroit outfielder Sam Thompson won the NL batting crown with a .372 batting average that season, and led the league with 166 runs batted in (RBIs). When the Wolverines folded two years later, Thompson became a Philly.

Thompson was soon joined in the Philadelphia outfield by Ed Delahanty and "Sliding" Billy Hamilton. The three of them formed one of the greatest outfield combinations of all time.

Ed Delahanty was the oldest of five brothers, who all played in the major leagues. He was one of the finest hitters of the nineteenth century. In his 13 seasons with the Phillies, Delahanty led the league in doubles 4 times, RBIs 3 times, and home runs (HRs) twice. His .346 lifetime batting average ranks fourth on the all-time list.

The Phillies offense was the most potent in all of baseball from 1892-1895. Thompson, Hamilton and Delahanty all batted over .400 in 1894. The Phillies' team-batting average of .349 that season remains the highest ever recorded. Unfortunately, the Phillies also had one of the league's worst pitching staffs. They never finished higher than third place.

Billy Hamilton was traded to the Boston Beaneaters after the 1895 season. He later rejoined Harry Wright, Sam Thompson, and Ed Delahanty in the Baseball Hall of Fame.

Pitcher Grover Cleveland "Pete" Alexander won 373 major league games in his career.

Grover's Era

Grover Cleveland "Pete" Alexander joined the Phillies in 1911, and led the NL in wins with 28 in his rookie season. It was the first of many records he would earn in his 20 seasons as a major league pitcher.

Alexander was the NL's winningest pitcher again in 1914 with 27 wins. The following season, he began his incredible string of pitching Triple Crowns, leading the NL in wins, earned run average (ERA), and strikeouts for three straight seasons from 1915-1917.

The Phillies' offense was powered by Clifford "Gavvy" Cravath. He won six NL home run crowns while playing outfield for the Phillies. His league-leading 24 HRs and 115 RBIs, combined with Alexander's Triple Crown pitching of 31 wins, a 1.22 ERA, and 241 strikeouts brought Philadelphia its first NL Pennant in 1915.

The Phillies faced the Boston Red Sox in the 1915 World Series. Alexander defeated Boston in Game One by a score of 3-1, and Philadelphia jumped out to an early series lead. The next four games were pitching duels, each decided by a single run. The Phillies lost all four, and the Red Sox became World Champions.

The Phillies would not return to the World Series for another 35 years. They traded Alexander, the most dominating pitcher in baseball, to the Chicago Cubs, before the 1918 season.

Pete Alexander won 373 Major League games in his career. He ranks third on the all-time list behind Cy Young (511) and Walter Johnson (417). He is the NL's all-time leader in shutouts, with 90, and complete games with 437. Grover Cleveland "Pete" Alexander was elected to the Baseball Hall of Fame in 1938.

Phillies' outfielder Cy Williams poses for photographers prior to a game with the New York Giants in 1923.

Radio Days

When the Phillies won their first NL Pennant in 1915, the only way to find out about a ball game was to go to the stadium, or read about it in the newspaper. Radio was a fairly new invention, and it was not yet being used to broadcast entertainment. By the time the Phillies returned to the World Series, it was seen by more than 38 million Americans on another new invention, television.

During baseball's radio days of the 1920s, '30s, and '40s, the Phillies were the worst team in baseball 17 times! They were not without great players, however.

The Phillies' home games were played at the Baker Bowl, before the team moved into Shibe Park (later called Connie Mack Stadium) in 1938. The right-field corner at the Baker Bowl was only 281 feet from home plate, giving many left-handed hitters cause for excitement.

Cy Williams came to the Phillies in 1918. The left-handed outfielder won NL home run crowns in 1920, 1923, and 1927. Philadelphia finished last in the NL all three years.

Francis "Lefty" O'Doul spent two seasons in the Baker Bowl outfield. He won an NL batting crown with the Phillies in 1929. O'Doul's 254 hits that season broke Rogers Hornsby's NL single-season record. It remains second on the all-time list behind George Sisler's AL mark in 1920 with 257.

Perhaps the best Phillies player, during these disastrous three decades, was Chuck Klein. Another left-handed batter, Klein led the NL in home runs four times in his first six years with the Phillies. He was the NL's Most Valuable Player (MVP) in 1932, as the Phillies enjoyed a winning season for the first time in 15 years.

The following season, Philly catcher Virgil "Spud" Davis finished second in the NL with a .349 batting average. Klein won the NL Triple Crown the same year with 28 HRs, 120 RBIs, and a .368 batting average. The 1933 Phillies, meanwhile, had the worst pitching and fielding in the league, dropping them back near the bottom of the NL Standings.

Just as Pete Alexander before him, Klein's Triple Crown season was followed by his trade to the Chicago Cubs. He returned three years later, and finished his career as a member of the Phillies in 1944. Chuck Klein was inducted into the Baseball Hall of Fame in 1980.

Whiz Kids!

The Phillies came under the ownership of Robert M. Carpenter in 1943. His son, Robert Jr., became team president, and hired Herb Pennock as general manager.

Pennock was a former pitcher with Hall-of-Fame credentials. He quickly went to work, building a minor league farm system to develop talent for the Phillies. Herb Pennock died in 1948. His farm system produced a corps of young players who became known as Philadelphia's "Whiz Kids."

The Phillies finished last again in 1947, but help was on the way. Curt Simmons, a left-handed pitcher, was brought up late in the season. Simmons was joined on the Phillies' pitching staff by rookie right-hander Robin Roberts in 1948. Before long, Roberts and Simmons would become one of the most devastating right-left combinations in baseball history.

Richie Ashburn was another Philly rookie in 1948. The fleet-footed center fielder led the league in stolen bases with 32, and finished second with a .333 batting average his first season. Even more outstanding was Ashburn's ability to track down long fly balls.

By 1950 the Phillies looked as though they would cruise to their first NL Pennant in 35 years. Del Ennis paced the offense, leading the NL in RBIs with 126. Stellar relief pitching by veteran Jim Konstanty boosted the starting performances of Simmons and Roberts. Konstanty picked up 16 wins and 22 saves, coming out of the bullpen to earn the 1950 NL MVP Award.

Facing page: Phillies' pitcher
Robin Roberts in action.

With just two weeks left in the season, the Phillies held a seven-game advantage. The onset of the Korean War caused Curt Simmons to be called for military duty.

The Phillies lost two more of their starting pitchers, Bob Miller and Bubba Church, to injuries. They began to be called the "Fizz Kids," as their hold on the NL lead began to slip, and the Brooklyn Dodgers quickly closed ground.

The Dodgers were one game behind when they hosted the Phillies in the season finale at Ebbetts Field. Robin Roberts was the Phillies starting pitcher for the fourth time in eight days. Brooklyn countered with Don Newcombe. Each pitcher had won 19 games, as they approached the final NL match-up of 1950.

The score was tied in the bottom of the ninth inning, when the Dodgers put two men on for Duke Snider. With no outs, Philadelphia expected the slugger to lay down a bunt. "The Silver Fox" swung away, lashing a single to center. As the winning run rounded third, Ashburn fielded the ball and threw a perfect strike to home plate.

Rescued by Ashburn's throw, Roberts sent the game to extra-innings. The Phillies put two men on in the tenth, and with one out Dick Sisler stepped to the plate. Sisler was down to his last strike, when he lined Newcombe's fastball into the left field seats for a three-run homer! Roberts was perfect in the bottom half of the inning, and the Whiz Kids had won it!

The 1950 NL Pennant was the Phillies second in 67 years of baseball. It would have to be enough for Philadelphia fans. The New York Yankees swept the pitching-plagued Whiz Kids to win their second World Championship in a row.

It would be another 30 years of waiting before the Phillies returned to the World Series. From 1952 to 1955, Robin Roberts led the NL in wins. Richie Ashburn won two NL batting crowns for the Phillies in 1955 and 1958. Neither player ever returned to the post-season. Both were inducted into the Baseball Hall of Fame.

Dick Allen steps up to the plate.

Spoilers

By the end of the 1950s, the Phillies had sunk back to the bottom of the NL. They remained there four straight seasons, before rising to seventh place in 1962. The era of the Whiz Kids was gone, as new manager Gene Mauch attempted to revive the Phillies' hopes for a championship.

Dick Allen became the full-time third baseman for the Phillies in 1964. He led the NL in triples and runs in his rookie season. Allen's outstanding production earned him the 1964 NL Rookie of the Year.

Leading Philadelphia's pitching staff was Jim Bunning. In his nine seasons with the Detroit Tigers, Bunning had been an AL All-Star five times.

Everything seemed to be going the Phillies' way in 1964. On June 21, Jim Bunning pitched a perfect game at New York's Shea Stadium. It was the first perfect game tossed in the NL since 1880!

By August, the Phillies had built a large lead in the NL Pennant race. They were 10 games in front of the competition, with just 3 weeks remaining. That is when the "Phutile Phillies" began to collapse.

With 10 straight losses down the stretch, the Phillies' pennant hopes were dashed. The St. Louis Cardinals and Cincinnati Reds quickly made up ground as time ran out. Philadelphia was reduced to the role of spoiler, as they defeated the Reds in the final two games of the season. The Cardinals took the 1964 NL Pennant. The Phillies and Reds finished tied for second, one game behind.

Jim Bunning, shown in a typical pitching sequence, here during the sixth inning when he pitched a perfect game against the New York Mets June 21, 1964. The Phillies won 6–0.

Steve Carlton delivers a pitch against the New York Mets.

Lefty's Era

Major League Baseball expanded and divisional play began in 1969. In 1971, the Phillies moved into Veterans Stadium. Before the end of the decade, Philadelphia would become a force in the NL East.

The Phillies traded for Steve "Lefty" Carlton in 1972. In his first year with the club, Carlton performed a pitching Triple Crown, leading the NL with 27 wins, 310 strikeouts, and a 1.97 ERA. Somehow, Philadelphia managed to finish in last place. Carlton accounted for nearly half of the Phillies 59 victories, and won his first NL Cy Young Award.

Mike Schmidt became the Phillies regular third baseman in 1973. Again, the Phillies finished last. The next season, Schmidt won the first of his eight NL home run crowns and Philadelphia began to climb out of the basement.

In 1975, the Phillies rose to second place in the NL East. Greg "The Bull" Luzinsky paced the NL with 120 RBIs, while Schmidt took his second home run crown with 38 in as many years. Beginning in 1976, Luzinsky, Schmidt and Carlton would lead the Phillies to three straight NL East Titles!

Philadelphia

Outfielder Cy Williams won NL home run crowns in 1920, 1923, and 1927.

Pitcher Grover Cleveland Alexander led the NL with 28 wins in his 1911 rookie season.

Dick Allen, 1964 NL Rookie of the Year.

From 1952 to 1955, Hall-of-Famer Robin Roberts led the NL in wins.

Phillies

Steve Carlton came to the Phillies in 1972, the year he won his first NL Cy Young Award.

Greg Luzinsky led the NL in 1975 with 120 RBIs.

In 1976, Mike Schmidt won a Gold Glove Award.

In 1993, Lenny Dykstra scored more runs than any NL player since Philly Hall-of-Famer Chuck Klein in 1932.

Schmidt added a Gold Glove Award to his third straight NL home run crown in 1976. He would go on to win the honor, as the NL's top fielding third baseman, 10 times in his career!

Carlton picked up his second NL Cy Young Award in 1977. Using a devastating slider, Lefty was compiling strikeouts on a record-breaking pace.

The NL Pennant remained elusive. The Phillies were swept by Cincinnati's "Big Red Machine" in the 1976 National League Championship Series (NLCS). The following two years, the Los Angeles Dodgers represented the National League in World Series play.

After falling to fourth place in 1979, the Phillies began the new decade with a fourth NL East Title. Mike Schmidt was the overwhelming choice for the NL MVP Award, as he completed the finest season of his outstanding career with 48 HRs and 121 RBIs. Carlton won his third NL Cy Young Award.

Frank "Tug" McGraw, a 15-year veteran of Major League Baseball, recorded 20 saves for the Phillies in 1980. Pete Rose, baseball's all-time leader in hits, played his second season as a Philly. Rose left the Cincinnati Reds through free-agency in 1979. This time, the Phillies defeated the Houston Astros in the NLCS to win their third NL Pennant in team history.

Left: Mike Schmidt dives to catch a hard ground ball. *Facing page:* Greg Luzinski hits a homer in a game against Montreal.

Philadelphia met the Kansas City Royals in the 1980 World Series. Neither team had ever won the "Fall Classic." The series went six games. Tug McGraw picked up a win and two saves coming out of the bullpen. After 97 years the Phillies finally overcame their demons to become baseball's World Champions!

Steve Carlton won a record-breaking fourth Cy Young Award in 1982. The following season, the Phillies returned to the World Series. After taking the NL East for the fifth time in eight years, they defeated the Los Angeles Dodgers in the 1983 NLCS.

John Denny became the new ace of the Phillies pitching staff that season. Denny led the NL with 19 wins and earned the 1983 NL Cy Young Award. Denny and Carlton combined to win only one game in the 1983 World Series. The Baltimore Orioles defeated Philadelphia in five games.

Mike Schmidt won a second NL MVP Award in 1986. Three years later, he retired from baseball. Schmidt currently ranks seventh on baseball's all-time list with 548 home runs. He became a member of the Hall of Fame in 1995.

Steve Carlton left the Phillies in 1986, and retired two years later. He ranks second on the all-time list with 4,136 strikeouts. He is the second winningest left-handed pitcher in baseball history behind Warren Spahn. Lefty Carlton entered the Baseball Hall of Fame in 1994.

Facing page: John Denny winds up for a delivery in a 5–1 win over the New York Mets. *Right:* Tug McGraw hurls a pitch during the 1980 World Series against Kansas City.

Worst To First

The Philadelphia Phillies have finished in last place more than any other team in NL history. By the end of the decade, in which they won their first World Championship, the Phillies were back in the cellar of the league's standings.

In 1992, the Phillies had one of the worst records in all of baseball. They finished last in the NL East for the third time in five seasons. But the following year, Philadelphia won its fifth NL Pennant!

The 1993 Phillies won with a group of the wildest characters ever assembled on one team. First baseman John Kruk exemplified the look. Appearing more like a truck driver than a ballplayer, Kruk displayed a total disregard for fitness. With his belly protruding over his belt, and long hair and beard flowing from his cap, he still finished among the league leaders with a batting average of .316.

If Kruk had the look, Lenny "Nails" Dykstra showed off the Phillies' hard-nosed style. Batting lead-off for Philadelphia in 1993, Dykstra scored more runs than any NL player since Philly Hall-of-Famer Chuck Klein in 1932. "Nails" finished second in the NL MVP voting, behind Barry Bonds.

Facing page: Phillies' relief pitcher Mitch Williams relaxes during a workout.

The Phillies got off to a fast start in 1993, and carried their lead in the NL East from wire-to-wire. In the NLCS, they faced the Atlanta Braves. Atlanta was favored in the series, having won the NL Pennant in the previous two seasons. But the self-proclaimed "Dirtbags" from Philadelphia dispatched the clean-shaven Braves in six games!

Mitch Williams converted a club-record 43 saves for the Phillies in 1993. The left-hander's throwing motion included falling off the mound after every pitch. His erratic style and general lack of control earned him the nickname "Wild Thing." Williams blew two save opportunities in the NLCS, but each time the Phillies came back to give him the victory. In the World Series, "Wild Thing" was not as fortunate.

The Toronto Blue Jays returned to the World Series as defending World Champions. They took a three-games to one advantage over the Phillies when Williams blew a save in the highest-scoring contest in World Series history (15-14). The Phillies came back to win Game Five, as Curt Schilling pitched a five-hit shutout. In Game Six, the "Wild Thing" returned.

First baseman John Kruk bats in the early innings of the Phillies' 1994 home opener against the Colorado Rockies.

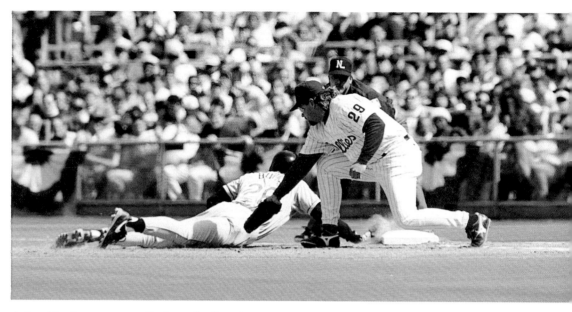

John Kruk tags out Colorado Rockies' Ellis Burks during the Phillies' 1994 home opener. Kruk rejoined the team after undergoing surgery and treatment for cancer.

In the seventh inning, Dykstra blasted his fourth home run of the series, and the Phillies scored five times to regain the lead 6-5. Needing a win to survive, manager Jim Fregosi called on Williams to save the game in the ninth.

"Wild Thing" promptly walked Ricky Henderson on four pitches. One out later, he gave up a single to Paul Molitor. Joe Carter followed, and did something that had only been accomplished once before. His three-run blast into the left field seats ended the World Series.

After his best season, Williams' career was effectively over. He was traded shortly after the World Series loss, and has made precious few appearances since.

A New Look

John Kruk was diagnosed with cancer in 1994, and retired from baseball a year later. Lenny Dykstra continues to be the Phillies spark-plug. And free-agent Gregg Jefferies signed with the Phillies in 1995. Philadelphia's All-Star catcher, Darren Daulton, has undergone knee surgery six times, but vows to return.

Major League Baseball expanded further in 1994, realigning each league into three divisions. The Phillies remain in the NL East, where they must now contend with the World Champion Atlanta Braves.

The Philadelphia Phillies have five NL Pennants to their credit, but have won the World Series only once. They have over 100 years of baseball history behind them. Today, the Phillies continue in their quest to double their World Championship total.

Lenny Dykstra at bat against the New York Mets.

Glossary

All-Star: A player who is voted by fans as the best player at one position in a given year.

American League (AL): An association of baseball teams formed in 1900 which make up one-half of the major leagues.

American League Championship Series (ALCS): A best-of-seven-game playoff with the winner going to the World Series to face the National League Champions.

Batting Average: A baseball statistic calculated by dividing a batter's hits by the number of times at bat.

Earned Run Average (ERA): A baseball statistic which calculates the average number of runs a pitcher gives up per nine innings of work.

Fielding Average: A baseball statistic which calculates a fielder's success rate based on the number of chances the fielder has to record an out.

Hall of Fame: A memorial for the greatest baseball players of all time located in Cooperstown, New York.

Home Run (HR): A play in baseball where a batter hits the ball over the outfield fence scoring everyone on base as well as the batter.

Major Leagues: The highest ranking associations of professional baseball teams in the world, currently consisting of the American and National Baseball Leagues.

Minor Leagues: A system of professional baseball leagues at levels below Major League Baseball.

National League (NL): An association of baseball teams formed in 1876 which make up one-half of the major leagues.

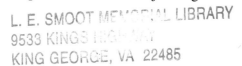
L. E. SMOOT MEMORIAL LIBRARY
9533 KINGS HIGHWAY
KING GEORGE, VA 22485

 29

National League Championship Series (NLCS): A best-of-seven-game playoff with the winner going to the World Series to face the American League Champions.

Pennant: A flag which symbolizes the championship of a professional baseball league.

Pitcher: The player on a baseball team who throws the ball for the batter to hit. The pitcher stands on a mound and pitches the ball toward the strike zone area above the plate.

Plate: The place on a baseball field where a player stands to bat. It is used to determine the width of the strike zone. Forming the point of the diamond-shaped field, it is the final goal a base runner must reach to score a run.

RBI: A baseball statistic standing for *runs batted in.* Players receive an RBI for each run that scores on their hits.

Rookie: A first-year player, especially in a professional sport.

Slugging Percentage: A statistic which points out a player's ability to hit for extra bases by taking the number of total bases hit and dividing it by the number of at-bats.

Stolen Base: A play in baseball when a base runner advances to the next base while the pitcher is delivering a pitch.

Strikeout: A play in baseball when a batter is called out for failing to put the ball in play after the pitcher has delivered three strikes.

Triple Crown: A rare accomplishment when a single player finishes a season leading the league in batting average, home runs, and RBIs. A pitcher can win a Triple Crown by leading the league in wins, ERA, and strikeouts.

Walk: A play in baseball when a batter receives four pitches out of the strike zone and is allowed to go to first base.

World Series: The championship of Major League Baseball played since 1903 between the pennant winners from the American and National Leagues.

Index

L.E. SMOOT MEMORIAL LIBRARY

3 1150 1002 6686 1

J   Sehnert, Chris W.
796.357   Philadelphia
64   Phillies
Seh   WITHDRAWN

L. E. SMOOT MEMORIAL LIBRARY
9533 KINGS HIGHWAY
KING GEORGE, VA 22485

L. E. SMOOT MEMORIAL LIBRARY
9533 KINGS HIGHWAY
KING GEORGE, VA 22485